ARABIAN MOONS

COLLECTION OF ARABIAN SHORT STORIES

AATHEEF RAHMAN

ISBN 979-888503685-6

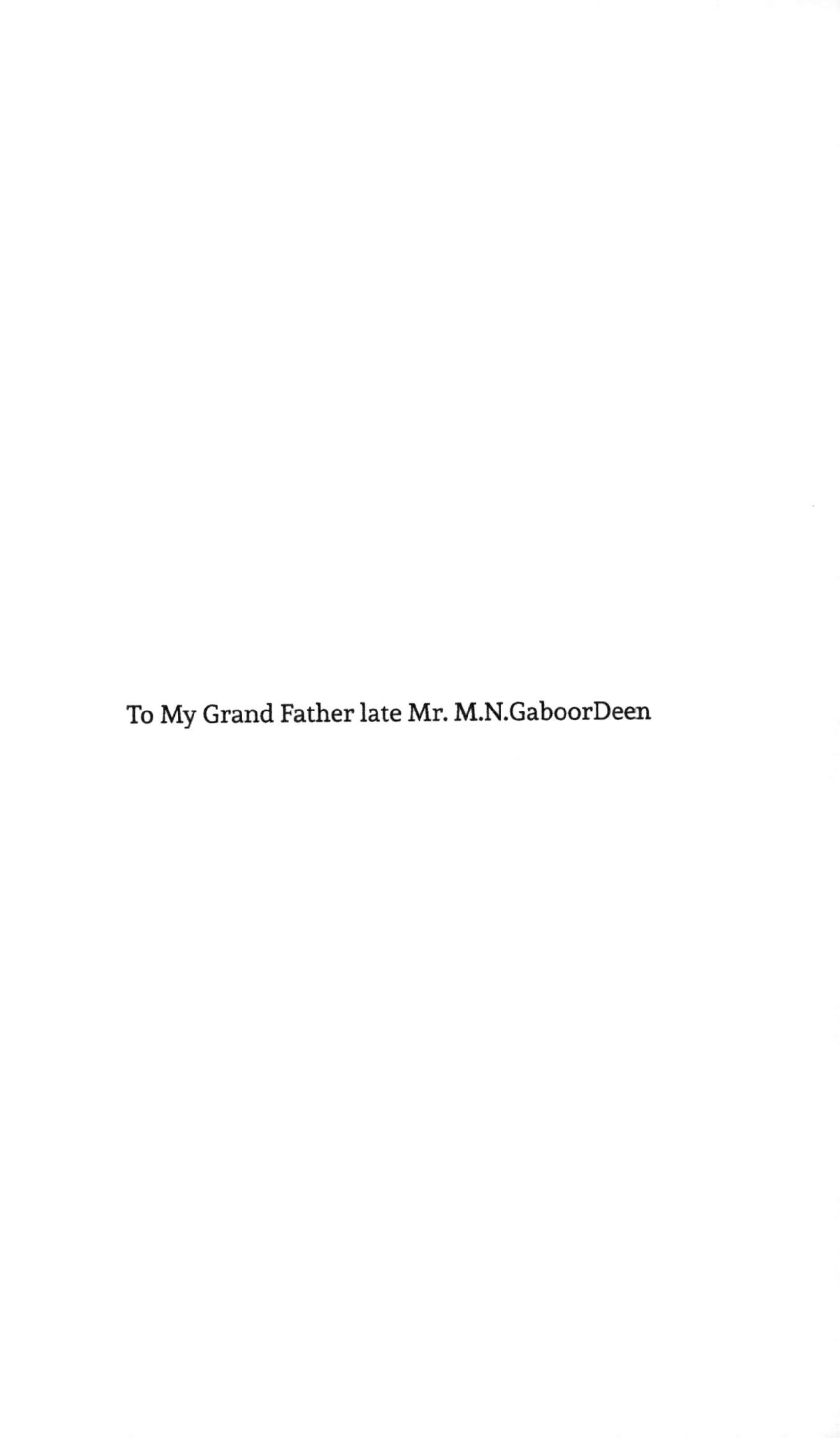

To My Grand Father late Mr. M.N.GaboorDeen

Contents

Contents

FOREWORD

We are also reminded of the Arabic tales of the Sindhabad tales of a thousand nights and the miracle of Alauddin, Alibaba and the Forty Thieves.

Here we do not find contemporary Arabic short stories in a position to receive attention. Even though we happen to see it on websites, it is often the environment that makes it impossible to read and enjoy it fully.

It is my desire and my mother's brother and writer Hidayatullah's desire that our Tamil readers should also select some good stories to translate into Tamil and consume the scent of Arabic literature in order to overcome that shortcoming.

The first step is to select some good stories under the names of the respective writers

I would like to compile in English and then publish in Tamil.

I hope that through this the Indian readers of various states will also have the opportunity to feel the current of contemporary Arabic literature.

PREFACE

By bringing my nephews into the habit of reading, I want to impress today's younger generation with the habit of reading.

It is commendable that in today's world it has facilitated book-making, literary service, and publication in multilingualism.

So I ask that we all use it not only to express our talents but also to show them to others.

Need to read a lot. Need to learn. Need to teach others. At least sharing experiences is good.

We need to make a further literary revolution in our language world as well.

Brothers and sisters, pay attention. Opportunities abound around us. It is not right not to use them.

We will also benefit and introduce ourselves to others. We must live as role models for the new generation.

The editor's job is almost a new experience for me.

It is truly commendable that this Notion Publication has made that opportunity possible through its software.

'Writter' Hithayadhulla.G

gaboordeen@gmail.com

Acknowledgements

At first I was not so interested in writing.

Admitting the truth, it can be said that it was my uncle Hithayadhulla who inspired me to write and to see it as a book.

They not only aroused curiosity but also introduced the Nossan Press, which operates quietly in the literary service.

And I remember with gratitude that he did all the work for this book for me.

I wonder when the urge to write was born.I am publishing my first collection with the desire to write.

I would like to thank my mother's elder brother and my uncle Hithayadhulla for effectively doing all the compilation work for this book.

I

Next Stop: Paradise

Written by Heba Arafa Mohamed Ali. (Egypt)

It was an icy-cold winter night. Silence reigned. Only the wind could be heard.

She turned her eyes to the sky. Clouds had rolled up and hidden the moon, which certainly didn't bode well.

Suddenly, her heart started racing. He was back. She could tell it was him, despite the darkness, because of his nauseating smell.

He threw a bucket of cold water over one of the girls knowing her screaming would wake up the rest. He then went to grab one of the younger girls, but she scooted away from him, running to hide behind her mother.

She, in turn, started pleading with him to have mercy on his own daughter, but that only seemed to enrage him. Without even bothering to try and verbalize his anger, he swung his rifle and smashed first the mother's and then the daughter's head with its butt.

The rest of the women started bellowing hysterically when they saw the blood gushing out of their friends' heads, but he didn't even flinch. Instead, he grabbed another one of the girls by the arm and left the room with her.

It wasn't until he was out of sight that Life could breathe again. She then started looking for her sister, but couldn't find her anywhere. That's when she realized it was her he had taken.

Her sister returned to the room about an hour later. Her nightgown was torn and blood-stained. She had her head down and was quivering badly.

Every step she took seemed to hurt her. She looked as if she were about to faint. Life helped her sit down on her mattress and checked her temperature.

She was burning hot and reeked of him, of evil incarnate. Seeing her sister so weak and morally crushed made Life wonder whether she would ever be able to recover.

And to think that those monsters were supposedly striving to make the world a better place, ruled by a fairer and more principled system...

The next night, she stayed awake, and when he returned, she made herself available to him. They went together to his tent and, the second he turned his gaze away from her, she took his gun, aimed it at him and pulled the trigger, all without a moment's hesitation.

She knew that the shot, with which she had tried to get some justice for the women who had been suffering the unspeakable day in and day out, couldn't have gone unnoticed, and since she couldn't risk being caught alive by his friends, she turned the weapon on herself, pressed its muzzle firmly against her chest, smiled—for revenge tasted sweet and she was positive she would wake up in Paradise the next morning, where she sure as hell had earned her place—and fired.

II

Till the Bitter End

Written by Mustafa Boualatin.(Algeria)

There are nineteen children inside the candle-lit church. They are sitting on the benches and enjoying a dinner consisting of broth, while chatting about the situation outside. They are not heeding Father John Paul's warning about chewing before swallowing. He goes to the statue of the Virgin Mary, kneels down in front of her and asks her to help him provide for the children.

Since its outbreak six years ago, the tuberculosis epidemic has wiped out one third of the city's population already. The first to die were the elders, who were then followed by the children.

The few who managed to survive the disease are now killing each other over the last scraps of food. As if that wasn't enough, the country has run out of oil. The wells that once dotted the desert have run dry. Hence, it is not safe to live here any longer.

Father John Paul made the right call, when, two years ago, he decided to turn Notre-Dame d'Afrique into a children's shelter.

He used to go out, scout the streets for homeless children who had been spared by the illness and offer them the church to stay at. That's how this family of twenty children between the ages of seven and fifteen came to be.

After dinner, they sit down in a circle to swap stories about their past lives and make up new ones about imaginary places, in order to escape from the harsh reality around them.

Father John Paul watches them, as their faces beam at times and crumple at others, while asking himself whether he is making a mistake by isolating them from the dog-eat-dog world outside, to which they will have to return eventually.

By shielding the children he has taken under his wing from all harm, is he ultimately not crippling them and dooming them to a lonely existence? Suddenly, he hears something. Unfortunately, it isn't just the drumming of the rain. No, it sounds more like approaching footsteps.

The kids have heard them as well. They immediately blow out all the candles, grab their rifles and crouch down under the benches. Silence ensues.

The door opens. Two grown men and a child are standing on the threshold. The child is Farid. His face is heavily bruised. He used to belong to them, but then he suffered a mental breakdown and left. That was four months ago.Lightning flashes, casting their long shadows on the church's tiles and lighting up the statue of Christ on the cross, the Virgin Mary, Saint Augustin and Margaret Berger.

"Show yourselves," one of them starts shouting, "we know you're hiding here somewhere. We promise we won't hurt you. We have just come to free you from this prison. Father John, it's time you acknowledged the end has come."

Father John Paul steps out into the light to face them. He has recognized the man's voice. He had once heard him preach at the mosque.

"These are my children and this is their home.

Here they have grown up and have learnt to become decent human beings, unlike your lot. Besides, nobody is forcing them to stay here with me."

As soon as he has finished talking, the children stand up and start shooting at the newly arrived party, riddling the three of them with bullet holes.

Their blood splashes on the church's walls and the plaque at the entrance, which reads, "Lady Africa, please guard us and our Muslim brothers from evil."

III

My City

The Author, Mohamed Naguib Tawfiq Hassan Matar: (Egypt)

The small city I call home lies on the Nile Delta. It's a very peaceful place, where the wind's moaning can be heard, and hence, everyone treasures silence. Most of its residents are either farmers or work at the local cotton ginneries.

The city, which is the capital of a province that includes several villages and is known for having been politically significant in the past, houses some schools and governmental buildings, and its edges peter out into bucolic countryside, where the warbling of birds and the crowing of cock fuses with the bray of ass and the grunts of camels, as well as with the yelling of the vendors on its streets.

The locals are good-faithed people who take life as it comes and don't fret over anything.

Their leave-for-tomorrow-what-cannot-be-done-today general attitude slows life down. Even the conversations they so effortlessly hold expand until it almost seems like they won't ever cease. Their carefree ways are certainly enviable. There is never a problem that is deemed too knotty to be solved.

Everyone is back from work by the time dinner is ready, at which point they gather around a big table to enjoy the superb food the women have cooked together.

After thanking God for all He hath bestowed on them, they go to bed. And they always sleep through the night. Whatever bane dogs them they handle with aplomb and patience, because they know their neighbors have their backs and will be there for them no matter what. Because no issue is to be taken so seriously that it may threaten straining relationships.

In winter, people take part in competitions for becoming the fastest and most dextrous one at sliding down mud slopes.

The mud, which has been carefully fixed in advance, starts to melt as soon as it is poured onto the roads because of how much heat they absorb during the day.

The contenders for the gold medal then wait in line, mentally rehearsing the choreography they are about to perform while sliding down the mud, which they are hoping will be remembered in the fashion of performances by the ballerinas at the Bolshoi company.

One of those cold winter nights—the mud almost dry already, the kids throwing stones at street lamps—the town's veterinarian arrived at the cowshed of one of the farmers.

His cow—his main source of income—had caught something and had been lying around, seemingly unable to get back on its hoofs, for the last two days. The veterinarian took the cow's temperature and, after taking a moment to examine it, drew the farmer to the side, as if he were trying to avoid being heard by the cow:

"If you wake up tomorrow morning and the cow's condition hasn't improved, slaughter it and sell the meat, before it goes bad and you are left with nothing."

The farmer asked teary-eyed, "Is there really nothing that can be done to save her?"

The veterinarian shook his head. The farmer was devastated.

What they didn't know, however, was that, while the cow had been successfully kept in the dark about her gloom fate, the sheep had heard everything. As soon as the coast was clear, they went to warn the cow of what might befall her if she didn't show signs of recovery by sunrise the next morning.

After all, the cow had always been kind to them and they knew she was mostly tired of working so hard. The cow thanked them for the tip-off and stood up at once, devoured all she could discern as edible around her and drained her water trough.

In the morning, the farmer went to check on the cow and found her standing and perked up. She had eaten all the food and drank the whole trough. He jumped for joy and praised the Lord saying:

"Oh God, let me repay you for your generosity with this offer: I will slaughter the sheep and feed the poor with their meat in your name."

IV

On the Inner Outsider

Written by Mohamed El Sharnoby.

I don't know why, but I am infatuated with this café, even though I didn't get what I came here for the first time I stepped inside.

In comparison, I felt like this eensy-weensy thingy, for the café is an institution nonpareil that provides a public forum for the locals, where they are welcomed to pour their hearts out without having to keep a civil tongue in their heads.

One has to be wary of being ripped off, though, for what is set on the tables tastes like sheer ambrosia for good reason: fancy don't come cheap. The fine sea views its windows give wound up prevailing on me and I sat down on one of its chairs and forked out some money for a drink.

I had just bought two books, mainly to look smarter than what my age made me seem. I was looking for someone with whom to engage in stimulating conversation and had been told to come here.

Time went by, but the increasingly-crowded café was doing little to match my expectations. Even straining my ears, I found it almost beyond the wit of man to catch any inkling of intellectual acuity that could reward my efforts to introduce myself to someone in the hopes they might turn into congenial company. I hence turned my head to the window and slipped into reverie, while trying to process the convivial atmosphere around me into background noise.

I see Alexandria as a museum, the one housing my past, and from where I was standing, it seemed like a fascinating one at that.

I have grown up now, and become driven but less feisty. I am an engineer who knows to choose his battles wisely. After all, there is no point in waxing lyrical about the world and what could have been done differently.

People are not interested in getting their heads churned by a maelstrom of philosophical questions, they just want a place to fritter time away and drown their sorrows, a place to belong no matter who they might be.

Looking out the window, I wondered whether the sea could be enjoyed the same from behind a sheet of glass. The noise inside the café had ceased bothering me. It almost sounded pleasing at this point.

After sitting there for an hour, I started feeling a bit woozy from the good-vibes ambience of the café and like locking gazes with strangers, including but not limiting to those in the scorching-hot outside world, scurrying by at the other side of my seat's window.

I finally decided it would do me good to fight my mingling weariness and foray into the hostile territory of social interaction.

From the exotic bamboo chairs and marble tables, to everything else contained or loitering in it, the café was complete eye-candy.

I looked up and tried to read meaning and insight into people's minds in the matrices the smoke they exhaled weaved when rising to the high ceiling. I wished the smoke could be more specific with its scurrilous allegations.

The babble of talk and the clatter of dishes and clinking glasses was joined by the clamor of street vendors, baying for customers.

The sun started sinking below the horizon and I felt betrayed; I hadn't been able to find anything nor anyone to keep me from wallowing in nostalgia, even though this specific café had looked like a promising alternative to frying in the boiling sun.

With the wisdom of hindsight, I believe I might not have entered the café that day seeking to discover a new way of looking at the world, which, in turn, begs the question as to whether the experience was worth the investment I made in it.

All I can say is that it made me feel less alone, less of a stranger to myself.

V

On Top of the Museum

Written by Mohamed Ibrahim. (Egypt)

All eyes were fixed on her. She was standing on the roof of the Egyptian Museum, right on top of the main entrance. Nobody knew how she had gotten there and she could barely remember it herself. She looked like she was about to jump.

One could tell the people on the ground were scared. They were running around like headless chickens. Some yelled at her that she should come to her senses and get down from there.

She was an unemployed widow without means to provide for her children. The country's spiraling inflation hadn't helped either.

She had heard people talk on the news about the loan Egypt was going to receive from the International Monetary Fund, as well as about Egypt's policy of letting its pound float free. She didn't have a clue as to what all that yapping was about, but she wondered why anyone would want them to starve to death. Then, one day, she felt tempted to murder her own children and have them for dinner.

That's when she realized she couldn't take it any longer. She had reached her breaking point.

Suddenly, the director of the museum showed up. He looked up at her and smacked both of his cheeks. He was positively distraught over what was going down. The publicity it would attract would be all but favorable. He didn't need an incident that might spark international outrage throwing him a curve, precisely now when things were going so well and the museum was finally receiving more foreign visitors thanks to how much the country's image had improved to outsiders.

All his worst fears stood confirmed seconds later, when a big group of tourists exited the museum, looked toward where everyone else was directing their gaze, and obviously, saw her.

In his desperation, he immediately clung to the hope that they might understand the woman's statement on the roof as another one of those unfathomable eccentricities that made Egypt so wonderfully exotic and that they would prefer to simply ignore it.

At least he didn't have to wait long to see his hopes shattered. One tourist started shouting hysterically in English straight away. At that moment, he wished the ground would swallow him up.

People kept pouring out of the building while a fire truck that had just popped up tried to force his way through the milling crowd of tourists. From above, the woman on the roof also spotted the arrival of men wearing fancy suits, dark sunglasses and stern expressions on their faces. As far as she was concerned, those men were nothing more than random bloodsuckers.

One was handed a megaphone. With an authoritative voice, he began to try and convince her to climb down from the roof. She, however, was not about to cave in just yet.

Minutes later, reporters for international news agencies started to flock to the scene.

They turned their backs toward her to face their camera crews before starting to elaborate on how well she exemplified how desperate people were because of how much more Egypt's economic policy had deteriorated its population's already dreadful living conditions.

More people in suits began to appear. Their previously inscrutable countenances started to bare their pent-up frustrations. Then, their designated spokesperson started to ask her for her demands. He was almost begging her to change her mind about committing suicide.

Suddenly, she recalled the movie Terrorism and Kebab. In it, the main character accidentally takes a building hostage.

When asked by the Minister of Interior to make his demands, he is unable to come up with anything he might want, despite lacking access to basic needs in his daily life. She felt like she had gotten into the same predicament the movie star's character finds himself in in that scene.

Time dragged. Every minute felt like an hour. The different groups formed by the assembled crowd were already fraternizing. Reality was slowly sinking in.

The second party of foreign journalists was joined by a third, a fourth, ...and then she lost count. And those were only the ones speaking a funny lingo! The amount of government officials had also multiplied tenfold with every new contingent at the scene insisting on taking charge of the operation.

The general mood was running high. She believed the heated passions that were creating the electric atmosphere down there were the ones to blame for the overly accelerated rate of the suits' proliferation.

Then the police arrived and cleared the place. However, cameras and cell phones kept flashing and recording from the other side of the police cordon. Most of their owners were probably already fantasizing with the number of views the exclusive material they were going to upload to the net next was going to receive.

Another reporter arrived with her crew, but this one—she noticed—didn't start jawing right away. As she witnessed the rather pitiful spectacle, a smile flickered across her face. She was enjoying it.

The growing throngs of onlookers were blocking the pedestrian traffic on Tahrir Square and its adjoining streets. From up there, it almost looked as if a zombie epidemic had struck the area.

By then, half the people down there couldn't see much and were left to wonder what was going on, and since the masses lust for blood, the rumor that all hell had broken loose in West Cairo started being spread via phone calls and had soon swept the city.

The voice on the megaphone asked her again, politely still, to put an end to the situation. Looking down at the amount of formally dressed men gathered on the ground, she surmised that people who were high up on the social hierarchy weren't really concerned about losing their jobs.

She liked to watch them in their helpless condition. A mocking smile spread across her face. Suddenly, she realized she had forgotten her reason for standing there.

VI

The Bath of the Damned

Written by Wafa Abdel-Lawi.(Algeria)

Once upon a time, something happened in this neck of the woods, the memory of which still plagues the locals to this day. Despite knowing, by all accounts, it's best not to dredge up the past, I am going to relay to you the episode that marked a before and after in this town's history on a night similar to this one.

This is the story of a young man who possessed all the desirable attributes of a Sir Galahad.

One day, his father, who was the chief of the biggest tribe in the region, which, thanks to its fertile land, made for a very comfortable and care-free life, fell seriously ill and died abruptly. Hence, the tribe elders assembled and, after a long meeting, decided that they would only agree to name the latter chief's son—the hero of our story—his successor on one condition: On the day of his nomination as chief, he would have to marry a woman they deemed his equal.

The problem with that condition was that our hero was all of a sudden really pressed for time, more so considering that there weren't any women around those parts who came even close to meeting the bar the elders had set for the prospective candidates to become his wife.

Panic broke out in our hero's family, who didn't want to relinquish power. Hence, they sat down to confer among themselves and find a solution to their problem. A large chunk of time went by before anyone came up with something other than a preposterous suggestion. It was an old man who spoke at that point, saying, "The only way you'll be appointed chief is if you commit incest."

Everyone looked at each other with furrowed brows. "What does he mean with 'incest'?", someone whispered. The grandmother, always so wise and in the know, was the one to raise her voice next:

"Everyone knows there is no lady far and wide who, regardless of her genetic or acquired endowments, will suit the elder's requirements for his future wife, but his own little sister, the most beautiful flower anyone has ever laid eyes on. We don't customarily marry our siblings, but you are not just anyone among us."

One could read in the faces of the congregated family members that Grandmother had helped dispel all doubts over what was at play. The elders had placed our hero between the devil and the deep blue sea. He knew he had to prove himself as a leader, and thus, stood up and went to the elders to announce his decision.

"I will marry my sister and you will kneel down and pledge obedience to me as your new chief."

Many were repulsed by his choice and decided to leave the tribe stating that marrying one's own sibling went against nature and would enrage God, who, in turn, would punish them all.

The night of his investiture as tribe chief, he was betrothed to his sister. Both wore their finest apparel. The feast that had been prepared by the women was a grand success and the food was praised to the heavens by all in attendance. Everyone danced their feet sore and had a great time at their nuptials. Suddenly, however, as if they had been standing over a volcano all along, the earth under them burst apart and lava flooded the place.

Everything and everyone turned to stone in a matter of seconds. The area they had been partying on right before hence became a forest of funny-looking petrified human sculptures.

The bodies of all those who assented to and witnessed the mental aberration that wedding represented have to this day remained the same way as they were on the fateful night their owners met their Maker. They have lost their eyes though, which melted when the red sea of fire reached them.

The waters that run through this stone graveyard are said to have healing properties. The sight looks pretty ghastly and, the locals, who are, though chary of telling it, still cognizant of the story behind the place's rock formations, call the area the Bath of the Damned.

VII
The Martyrs' Wall

Written by Yosef Hadday.(Iraq)

"And they found therein a wall about to collapse, so al-Khidh restored it."

It is fall and early in the morning. I have left the house to go to work. I know exactly what I will find every step of the way, for I have been following the same route every day for the last five years.

Just across from where I live, stands a pumping station. In front of its iron gate, sits the compound's security guard, who is always on the alert for intruders. I greet him, continue walking and pass by Sulman's and Hasan's workshops, the blacksmith and the carpenter.

I then cross the muddy area verging on the city park and my shoes get dirty. I reach the garage with the white fence, whose paint has started to flake. Next to it, stands a wall that is covered with pictures of martyrs. Most of them are wearing military uniforms, carrying guns and smiling. Some have even been portrayed leaning against tanks.

They appear to be glowing.

I greet them as well, like always. Suddenly, I notice there is a new picture hanging from the wall. I get closer to it and read its caption.

"Musa Naim died a heroic death fighting for his country and his beliefs in Gat."

I immediately feel the urge to ask the guy in the picture whether he has been killed by a sniper, in close combat or by an explosive device.

There is another picture glued to the wall that not only specifies the guy's name and the day he died, but also how he departed this world. Apparently, he was shot in the head and thrown into the river from a cliff along with many others while unarmed and trying to flee. Thanks to the current, which dragged his body away until it reached the territories controlled by the government, he was later found and given a proper burial.

I used to know one of the guys whose picture can be seen on the wall from back in the day. He used to be a real head-turner and a total hit with the ladies. Even now, after his death, girls stop to gawk at his picture. Some even shed a tear or two for all of the beauty that has gone to waste with his tragic demise.

And then, there is the picture of Abu Karar, my old friend. He always used to carry a bullet in his pocket, in order to avoid being captured alive.

However, it seems like, last minute, he backed out, unable to pull the trigger, for he was later beaten up and paraded around town by the enemy, before being hanged by the neck from a bridge. At the very least, we made sure he was avenged.

The story the pictures tell may not pride itself on the fancy words and slick imagery philosophers and poets use, but I think it still manages to resonate with all of us, as it is that of human suffering.

VIII

I Asked You, My Love

Written by Nourhan Abdallah.(Lebanon)

I was sitting in a small coffee shop with my laptop, listening to Fairuz sing, "I asked you, my love, where are we going? Let us be, let us be, and the years threw us off their scent." I checked my email from time to time. On TV, the 2006 war of Israel against Lebanon was being broadcasted. I therefore remembered Jakhour, the young lad living in the south of Lebanon.

He was also the brother of my Lebanese friend, Reema, whom I talked to every now and then. Our friendship had brought me closer to him. In the end, I was talking to him every single day, every hour, sometimes even every minute.

We fostered and cemented our relationship over time. The idea was for us to start seeing each other over there, to be able to enjoy the most precious of times, but the siege of Lebanon was prolonged, the tensions between the countries escalated, and then the war erupted.

I described to him the magnitude of my passion for Fairuz and my commitment to the Lebanese mountains teeming with cedars as well as the rest of the tourist sights.

I said, "Hi."

"What's up?" he replied.

"I am worried. I fear for your safety with the war that is raging over there. Are you all right?"

"I am fine. You should stop tuning in to listen to the whir of combat aircrafts and the whistle of missiles. Your alarm clock shouldn't be blazoning the death of children and the indigence of bereaved mothers. You have had enough of that. Just know that I am okay. In a few days' time we'll be celebrating our victory!"

The word "victory" to us meant the ribbon of salvation. It would set me free to see him and my cherished Lebanon. I had some beautiful memories of my childhood and my teenage years. Back then, my father believed leaving Lebanon and running off to Egypt was the best way to escape the doomed future lying ahead of us. Meanwhile, my mother feared for our lives, and since I was her little sugar pie, she decided that we would stay in Egypt until the war had come to an end. We would not return before then. Jakhour and I had decided to get married, so just after the war ended, I set my sights on making the journey that would allow me to be together with him once again. However, my mother forbade my traveling, saying, "You are still too young. If you leave now, I won't be able to recognize you when you come back."

My mother's reaction shocked me. Why did she want me to marry an Egyptian? I tried many times to convince her that I loved Jakhour, but she didn't seem to get it. She clung on to her stance even though my father gave me all the freedom in the world to make up my own mind.

I tried to catch up with Jakhour over the phone but was unable to reach him. His phone was switched off. What was going on? Lebanon had just won the war against Israel and the whole nation was on cloud nine. I asked my dad for the opportunity to return in order to visit the house we used to live in. I was hoping that I would bump into Jakhour. My family and I were over the moon all the way there. I left Jakhour a message telling him that we were flying to Lebanon, but I did not receive a reply.

When we arrived, we found out that our old house had been razed to the ground. My mother felt an ache in her heart. My father stroked her shoulder lovingly and said, "Do not worry. All that matters is that we are fine and that we have a house in Egypt."

I phoned Reema, but nobody picked up. Jakhour's phone was still turned off. Suddenly, Reema called me. In tears, she said, "Jakhour is dead."

IX

A Message from the Lady of the Sea

Written by Moutaz Ben Hamid.(Libya)

I was in a café admiring a glorious sunset over a calm sea. Most of the people who had come to spend the day at Juliyana Beach had already left and I could just lean back and enjoy the peacefulness of the surroundings. The smell of grilled fish wafted out from the neighboring restaurants and through the café's old wooden-framed windows, even though there was no wind blowing that day.

I was reading a book about Libyan history, while listening to the classical music drifting from the café's speakers. Suddenly, I came across a paragraph that caught my attention:

"Legend has it that the Juliyana Beach owes its name to the older daughter of the English consul Libya had in 1850, who, apparently, was a spoiled blonde of unparalleled beauty. When she was just seventeen years old, she went out for a swim in the sea and drowned. The beach was renamed after her to keep her memory alive."

It was already night—and a rather dark one at that—by the time I set out to return home. I decided to walk, in order to have a chance to confer with the sea on how to steal beautiful stuff and get away with it.

At some point, I started feeling tired and I lay down on the sand, which had retained the sun's warmth. I then went on to count the stars in the sky, my eyes closed and I fell asleep.

Suddenly, I was woken up by the gentle brush of fabric on the bare skin of my legs. I looked up and saw a beautiful tall blonde girl wearing a translucent white dress. She fit the history book's description of the mythical chick who drowned at sea to a T. She smiled at me, then turned around and went into the water. She didn't even bother to take her clothes off.

She continued striding forward until it was just her head peeking out of the water, at which point she waved for me to join her in the ocean. Without waiting for me to make up my mind, she started swimming out to sea. Admittedly, I felt tempted to accept her proposal, but decided to decline it at the last minute. I wasn't ready for such a huge commitment.

However, right before disappearing out of sight, she started screaming for help, "Don't let me drown again! I am the love of your life, Juliyana, Benghazi, the ground under your feet!"

Enter Caption

I hurriedly took off my clothes to jump into the water. However, as I tried to run towards her, I realized that I was unable to move. While struggling to keep her head above water, she cried, "I beg you! Don't leave me here to die! You are my only hope! Call for help! I am counting on you!"

That's when I woke up. It was still nighttime, the tide had risen and waves were lapping my feet. I stood up and took a look around me. The beach seemed empty. I sighed. Juliyana's words were still ringing in my ears.

X

You are a fucking Christian

Written by Rehab Uthman Shanib.(Libya)

Naguib was sitting in front of the shop trying to shoo the flies away as black thoughts kept popping into his mind. They wouldn't be as easily scared off as the flies. Every time he succeeded in pushing one aside, another one ran in to take its place. "Looks like I am screwed," he said to himself and let out a long sigh of despair.

Suddenly, a man walking down the road notorious for leading to hell started singing softly, "Broken hearts wear long faces with vacant eyes."

He stopped in front of Naguib's shop and asked him, "What's up?"

Naguib snapped out of his trance and replied, "Everything's fine."

"This place looks like no man's land to me."

"That's because this is indeed no man's land."

Naguib's friend Muhammad, who was sitting in his car with his mother and sister, shouted to the man, "Naguib's this town's only king. That is beyond dispute."

Naguib smiled and said, "I beg to differ."

The man entered the shop and exited moments later with a pack of cigarettes and two bottles of water.

"God bless," he said before walking away.

The ceasefire had come into effect a few days before, and peace prevailed for the first time in forever. Even a few cars had started to drive past the area.

Interrupting her while she prayed, Muhammad's mother said to her daughter, "Your brother never misses out on an opportunity to get into trouble. At least you leave your mobile phone at home."

The girl nodded assent and resumed her prayers in silence. Muhammad decided to rejoin them while darting a look of complicity at Naguib. "It's not like we only use the phone to waste time slaughtering language via Facebook and Viber. It's also a reliable source of information, which given the delicate nature of the situation, is something that it never hurts to have so that one can brace oneself for what the future holds."

His mother opened her mouth to retort, but then Naguib nodded, settling the matter.

Right after leaving the house earlier that morning, Muhammad had told Naguib, "I just fed my sheep. They are yours in case anything happens to me. I trust you'll know how to keep them out of harm's way."

Most of the shops on the road to the cement factory in the al-Hawary district had closed down. It was only very recently that a few of the many grocers who used to dot the street had dared to go back to business. But Naguib was positive that the area would, albeit slowly, steadily return to life. There were some cars parked in front of the al-Hawary Hospital, and an oil factory had just opened. However, most of the chicken farm employees—mainly Egyptians—who used to swarm the street were nowhere to be seen anymore. The shops around the Jazeera Dauran roundabout, where only black workers could be sighted now, had all closed down as well. The fields had been abandoned and many houses had been razed to the ground by missiles.

Muhammad's mother asked her son, who had just been talking to someone on the phone, "Any news?"

He shook his head.

Naguib got into the car with the rest of the family, and they drove off to carry out the neighborhood patrol. A few moments later, they found an open shop. They stopped the car, went to the owner, greeted him, and told him, "So far everything looks calm. However, do not linger outdoors. Close early today. Just in case. Better safe than sorry."

Then they jumped back into the car and drove off. As they arrived at the Jazeera Dauran roundabout, Muhammad's sister suddenly screamed and asked them to stop the car. "I forgot my blood sugar meter!"

The prayers she uttered next were of a slightly different nature than the ones she had been sending up since she had left the house.

At the roundabout, a checkpoint had been set up and some masked men were searching the cars. The vehicles with families were rarely stopped for long. However, when their turn came, one of the men asked them to pull over to the side of the road. Naguib was asked to step out of the vehicle. Meanwhile, the family was asked whether Naguib belonged with them. Muhammad immediately answered, "Ain't it obvious?"

Finally, they were allowed to drive through, and they returned to Naguib's shop. They closed it for the day and started heading back home. The roads were empty and they could hear explosions in the distance. Then Muhammad and Naguib began quarreling. Naguib wanted to close the shop for good and leave the country, but Muhammad argued that it would be a dreadful mistake to relinquish their only source of income.

Desperate to find a way of making Muhammad understand the crux of the issue, Naguib said, “The Christian population is being massacred!”

Muhammad froze on the spot. Then he slapped his friend’s face. He looked at Naguib while trying to control the emotions that were churning inside him. Muhammad yelled in a voice breaking with anger, “You piece of shit! You are a fucking Christian!”

XI

Forever in the Seagull's Debt

Written by Ibn Allal Sidi Khaled.(Morocco)

Time stopped. My heartbeat started racing and I gasped for air. I felt like I was buried under debris.

It was as if I had just come across another layer of the human soul, which revealed itself wider than the sky and deeper than the sea standing in front of me. I never thought I would deliberately seek to face my worst nightmare!

The Seagull Shore is a beautiful beach on the Mediterranean coast which has yet to be discovered by outsiders. Only a few boats chug out to sea from the docks that can be found nearby. The women of the courageous sailors stay ashore, waiting anxiously for their safe return home. The shore is also frequented by youngsters, who go there to get high and stare at the horizon.

That beach is, in my eyes, the country's crowning glory. It brings me hope for the future. From there, one can discern Europe's coastline on a clear day. Europe, that promised land whose siren song has led so many to drown in sea. I have always wondered why the ground to the North of the Mediterranean is so much more covetable than the one to the South.

My gaze had fallen on a seagull and it suddenly seemed as if there was nothing else that mattered in the entire world but the feeling of belonging to the present time and the space surrounding me that the seagull gave me. Its eyes were glued to me. I thought it resembled a child wanting but not daring to ask an embarrassing question. I went towards it. It was perched on top of a four-meter-tall concrete wall rising not far from where I was standing. With my fear of heights, it seemed like it was going to be a breeze climbing the narrow wall and walking on it to get closer to my feathered friend! Ceasing to bother with it definitely seemed like the better idea, but I couldn't help wanting to discern its fixed, piercing and steely gaze, which had me completely riveted to the spot. The rest of the gulls seemed like drooling idiots in comparison. Hence, I took the stairs that led to the top of the wall and started inching towards it. I had to meticulously measure my every move to avoid scaring it away. Suddenly, my head started pounding and I started feeling dizzy. I had gotten as close as humanly possible. I felt relieved, like I had overcome my fears. Reality seemed to have acquired a new dimension thanks to that seagull's impenetrable eyes and inscrutable countenance.

XII

Impossible Love

Written by Amal Al Mahyoub.(Yemen)

Suad distractedly looked out the window of her room. She had loud music playing in the background, but she wasn't paying attention to the songs' lyrics. She absent-mindedly wound a lock of her black hair around her finger and ran the other hand over her face. Suddenly, a memory made her bronze cheeks redden.

Today was her little sister's wedding day. Her soon-to-be husband had been sending her so many gifts from the Emirates over the past few months that both Suad's and her sister's room had wound up piled with them. The warm winds that swept through the city at that time of year had just started blowing. Suad wondered whether she was destined to find happiness in life.

She lived at home with her parents. Her father worked at Aden's water purification plant and her mother had retired recently after spending 25 years teaching at a high school in Crater. She was proud of her forward-thinking parents, who had instilled confidence in her and allowed her and her sister to have a lot of freedom while growing up.

The aroma of black henna wafted toward her and made her hazel eyes drift over to the jar it had emanated from, which was standing on top of a wooden table. It brought back memories of her ex. Try as she had, she hadn't been able to get over him. He owned a stand of beauty products at the souk she had to traverse every day to get home from college. The first thing that struck her about him was his chilled manner and his elegant bearing, but what drove her to fall in love with him were the dialectical exchanges she had with him.

Shortly after first taking notice of him, she acquired the habit of stopping at his stand to buy a jar of henna on her way back home. She knew her fancy for him was reciprocated because she had caught him stealing glances at her and because of how he smiled at her.

Her taste in music and literature changed in a matter of weeks. She started listening to love songs a lot more often and found herself looking up romantic novels online. Her well-intentioned friends warned her that, taking his ethnicity and origin into account, they weren't meant to be, but she had already fallen for him and dismissed their remarks by affirming that the heart doesn't understand skin pigmentation or humble beginnings in accord with social norms or hierarchies. She didn't care that he came from an underprivileged family that lived in the poor neighborhood of Basateen nor for the fact that he hadn't been able to finish primary education, for his knowledge of the world was broad and their long phone conversations provided her an unfettered outlet for her fevered imagination. No matter what anyone said, she considered him her tall, black, handsome boyfriend.

However, a few months into their secret relationship, her parents found out that she was seeing a boy from a different race and all hell broke loose. Her life turned into a nightmare; her parents decided to forbid her from leaving the house and she became a prisoner in her own home.

A couple of days afterwards, she received a message on her phone that brought tears to her eyes. It was from him and it read, "Given the color of my skin, I probably should deny my feelings for you, but, then again, perhaps they are worth fighting for."

XIII
Foundered Reality

Written by Ahmad Al Haron. (Palestine)

The power was off and the night was cold and moonless. Silence prevailed; only the sobs of children and the whistle of bullets being fired in every direction dared to punctuate it. The Angel of Death had decided to sojourn in our town for an indefinite period of time and it seemed he had only just started making himself comfortable among us. We lit some candles and formed a circle around them. Our eyes were fastened on their faint glimmer. It was the only thing we felt we could derive a feeling of safety from and we sucked on it like unweaned babies.

I didn't understand how some had managed to fall asleep knowing that they very well might not wake up again in the morning. I switched on my portable radio, which had seen better days, and gently, started turning the tuning knob in hopes of receiving a signal, preferably a God-sent and auspicious one. I couldn't afford to be picky, though, for my old radio was hardly in a cooperative mood. The awful screeches it emitted told me that, at least, the problem didn't lie in the fact that the batteries had run out. Regardless, the truth was that I couldn't count on it to keep me company throughout that black and baleful night.

Suddenly, a volley of shots rang out and I felt a surge of panic. I pulled a blanket over my head and laid down to try and catch some shut-eye. I needed to escape conscious reality no matter what. Yet, I couldn't help having the thought that I looked like a mummy in its coffin and feared that I might actually turn into one if I fell asleep with that picture in my mind. I could hear the wind blowing and the sand it dragged pelting against the window. Then, a raging storm broke out and torrential rain began to lash down. My father still hadn't returned home and I was worried sick. He had gone out to herd the sheep hours ago.

All of a sudden, I heard the plaintive bleating of sheep. I wanted to stand up and open the door, but then I realized that I had actually managed to drift off to the land of Nod and that I would have to strangle my survival instincts to travel back to the harsh dimension of reality in which I didn't exercise any sort of control. It took time and effort, but I made it, and as soon as I opened my eyes, I flicked my lighter to look for any obstructions in my path and rushed to the door. My father was standing on the other side. He was soaking wet and shaking. I ushered him inside and offered him something to eat. My lighter's flint wheel had become too hot to handle and I had to switch hands in order to avoid burning my thumbs. After a short while, I suggested we climb up to the second floor of the house to improve our visibility of the battlefield and psych ourselves up for what lay ahead, but he dismissed this idea with a shake of his head. Instead, he beckoned me to step outside the house. I obeyed, but not without hesitation.

I opened the door once again and, to my surprise, I saw that the sheep were all gone. The wanton destruction wrought by the war had spooked them and driven them to run for their lives. One lamb was trapped in barbed wire and was bleating at the top of its lungs. I then turned around to look at my father and saw that he had been hit by a bullet and was lying dead on the ground. "At least now he has reached Heaven," I thought. "He doesn't have to run any longer."

I leaned back on a nearby palm tree and started crying; I was surrounded by corpses. I tried to recall who fired the first shot, but all that came to mind was an image of the blinding sun.

XIV
At the Tea Vendor's

The author, Kamel Esawy:(Sudan)

I sighed with relief, having made certain that I had not mislaid any of my bags, and then sat down to enjoy a well-earned cup of tea. After all, I had been strolling up and down the vegetable market for hours. The place was swarming with tea vendors. The smell of mint and cloves hung in the air, tantalizing the passers-by. The clientele was rather scarce considering the crowds the place usually attracts. Other than that, nothing seemed out of the ordinary, nothing qualified as visually entertaining. The day had barely begun and I didn't want to return home just yet, given that, as an unemployed man, the alternative was to twiddle my thumbs at home all day. Thus, I decided to kill time by trying to memorize the messages printed on billboards and other commercial signs. I let my eyes bounce from the ill-looking people who dragged their feet to the pharmacy to the tea vendors, who seemed to be involved in a lively discussion, on which I decided to barge in.

Suddenly, a bearded young man sat down next to me. The trousers he wore started way below his waistline and rope-like dreadlocks dangled from his head. He stuffed them into a tricolor cap and inserted a pair of earbuds firmly into his ears. Then, he started to sway to the beat only he could hear. I immediately felt intrigued by him, so I approached him with a smile, "May I listen through one of your earbuds?"

He answered with an even larger return smile, "It's hip hop. Do you like listening to hip hop music?"

I said, "sometimes," and he passed me an earbud.

I placed it into my left ear and started listening to the lyrics of the song. After a short while, I removed the earbud and asked the young man if he would play the last part of the song again.

My request was granted and, after hearing the same piece of the song for the second time, I returned the earbud to the young man and asked him, "Did you understand what the singer just stated?"

"I'm not sure what you mean."

"You don't seem to have a very profound knowledge of the English language," I blurted.

The young man looked a little embarrassed. He then justified himself by saying, "I understand some of the words, but not all of them."

"So you have just chosen this music because of its rhythm," I surmised.

"One could say so."

"And do you want to know what the song says?"

"Please, I can't wait."

"It goes, You're miserable, because you try to be a good God-fearing person. You would be better off as a motherfucker. As a result, you would live in the lap of luxury, women would throw themselves on you and pour delicious red wine directly down your throat. At least now you know what you have to do to prevent the mayor ending up in bed with your wife."

The young man became visibly uncomfortable, perhaps feeling that I was too much all up in his business. He asked, "Do you want to keep listening?"

I respectfully declined.

Then, the young man put his earbuds back in his ears and proceeded to meticulously untangle the wires, which had gotten caught on the tentacles that grew from his skull. He took his time, in silence, letting me know that he was not in the mood to resume our conversation. Afterwards, he stood up, paid the tea vendor for the tea he had drunk and left. My eyes followed him until he vanished from sight.

As I turned my gaze back to my surroundings, I saw that he had left his wallet behind, which must have slipped out of his trouser pocket and which was now resting on top of the chair where he had been sitting a moment ago. I opened it, hoping to find some sort of card with his address or his phone number written on it so that I could return it to him. I have to admit, though, that I was also dying to know what it contained. However, all I found inside was a condom and some uppers.

I folded the wallet and handed it over to the tea vendor, saying, "The guy sitting next to me dropped his wallet before leaving. Here, in case he returns." She remarked, "I wouldn't bet on it. By now, I should be opening a lost-and-found office considering all the stuff I've gotten to keep from what people have misplaced over the years."

As I set out to return home, I inadvertently started humming the snippet of the song I had just listened to. It had stuck in my head! Suddenly, I stopped humming. I had come to a dawning realization. I had forgotten my bags with all the groceries I had bought that day at the tea vendor's!

XV
Jasmine Garlands

Written by Muhammad Fateeh Zidany.(Syria)

The sun disappeared behind a haze of smoke. All I could hear was people screaming. The streets reeked of death.

The market was particularly crowded that morning, because Ramadan started the following day and all the shops would stay closed until sunset. I was idly looking at the passersby and the old olive tree that grows in the middle of the square. I was thinking about my kids and how they would grow up around that tree to become staunch advocates of altruism and staying true to one's roots. For once, I wasn't minding the noise and the bustle around me, because I appreciated people's happiness and excitement over the upcoming festivities.

There was a girl selling jasmine garlands on the street. Every time she managed to sell one, her face lit up and her eyes slid over to a colorful dress on display in the window of one of the shops on the opposite side of the street.My boy, who was standing beside me, asked me whether I would take him to the toy store later that day. I told him it would be my pleasure, in exchange for a hug and a kiss.

Suddenly, aircrafts showed up in the sky. The noise they created was deafening. Their presence constituted a most unexpected turn of events, because, to the best of my knowledge, a truce had been negotiated with the enemy not that long ago! We should have known better than to trust them, I thought.

The first thing I did was instruct my kid to run for cover. He went inside the stall in front of which we had been standing and crouched down under a table. I saw him cling to the outfit I had gotten him to wear for the holidays. At that moment, I wished he could sprout wings, like the aircrafts, though perhaps more joy-eliciting, to escape the war.

In a matter of seconds, bombs started falling from the sky. Panic broke out. The market was under attack. The world around us shook each time an explosive device was dropped and struck the ground. Suddenly, I was hit by a piece of shrapnel. Stones were raining down on us. Blood started gushing out of my body. I started to feel dizzy and realized that I was going to die there. My whole life flashed before my eyes. Next I saw some strange creatures wearing white blood-stained robes ascend to the skies. I wanted to follow them, but I was still too heavy to defy gravity. It felt as if the lights were being turned down. White and blue dots flickered before my eyes. And the noise, so much noise! At least, I was still alive. I gathered all my strength to try and stand up. I was bleeding from the head, forearm and hip. The sky was covered in smoke and the ground was carpeted with dead bodies. The whole market was in flames and the fire was spreading to the nearby rising buildings, many of which had been razed to the ground.

I started calling my son's name the moment I recovered a sense of where I was. I started sifting through the rubble as I yelled, in hopes of finding my sweet little boy. I could feel him close. I prayed to God for his life and stretched my arm for him to be able to reach me. I also asked the Angel of Death to take me instead.

Suddenly, I slipped and fell through a crevice in the ground. People came to help me stand up and I continued searching for my son. I heard people shouting to me from behind to turn around, but I didn't want to listen to them. I might have been severely wounded, but my son was still missing.

Then I stumbled on the body of the girl who had been selling jasmine garlands. It was smeared with blood. Her gaze seemed fixed on the dress I had caught her gaping at while still alive.The world started spinning. The aircrafts had returned.

XVI
Surprise, Surprise

Written by Ebaa Khatib.(Syria)

One day, Nour's sister-in-law showed up to her house while her husband was on a four-day business trip and told her that her brother was going to divorce her in a couple of days. She warned Nour that she was telling it to her in confidence and asked her not to disclose who she had received the news from to anyone. She assured her that she had decided to inform her because she liked her and thought she had a right to know in advance.

"Do you know why he might be doing this?" She asked her.

"No," Nour replied, "I actually can't believe he's doing this to me! How did you find out? Did he tell you?"

"No, I heard him talk to someone over the phone. I heard him say he's going to take you to the Shmemis castle, to the same spot where he proposed to you, to serve you with divorce papers. You're sure there's nothing you can do to make him change his mind? Come on, you must have had an inkling that it might come to this at some point. If, looking back, we can establish when your marriage started to tumble, we may be able to come up with a strategy to make him reconsider giving your relationship another go."

"I am trying really hard to remember any point in time in which I felt we were growing apart, but, for the sake of me, I can't think of one. There has been no change in our daily life that may justify this decision he's making. I have been feeling a little bit under the weather as of late, but that's been it! That's no reason to dump someone, is it?"

"Of course not, but resentment can slowly build up over time. I'll leave you to reflect on it and, please, if you get to talk to my brother about this, remember: you didn't hear anything from me."

Nour showed her sister-in-law to the door. Once alone, she sat down on a chair to digest the news. How was it even possible that she hadn't had a clue as to what he had been up to? Was he really such a dick, that he would go away to arrange everything so that he could, upon his return, divorce her and leave her high and dry? Nour stood up and started pacing up and down the room. Men were such pigs! No way she was letting him screw her over, though. She intended to empty all of their bank accounts and move with all her most prized possessions to her parents' house before he came back from his trip.

On the next morning, she packed her stuff and got on a bus leaving for Homs, which is where her family lived. They were surprised to see her arrive and started grilling her immediately after she told them the reason behind her visit. Her mother saw she had some bruising below one of her knees and asked her whether he hit her. Both her sisters blamed her for his decision. The older one ascribed the breakdown of Nour's marriage to her bad temper, and the younger one, to her wish to delay getting pregnant for the third time. Nour's neighbor assumed he had fallen in love with one of his work colleagues. Her neighbor's mother suggested he might have even married her on the side. Nour's friend surmised she had caught him redhanded with some floozie in their bedroom.

Three days later, Nour's husband returned home from his business trip. Seeing that she wasn't there, he called her on the phone, "Where are you? I was so looking forward to seeing you. I got a surprise for you!"

"Don't bother telling me. I know all about your little surprise! You want to divorce me, you ...!", Nour blurted.

"Divorce you? Why on earth would you say that?"

"Listen, ..."

"No, you listen," said her husband interrupting her. "I have managed to get you transferred to another school, one closer to home, so that you don't have to get up so early every morning and drive all the way up to Hama to teach there. Did I not promise you I would make it happen? Instead of telling you right away, I thought of breaking the news to you in a more romantic setting, like the Shmemis castle where I proposed. Sorry for spoiling the surprise."

XVII
Je suis Bardo

The Author, Othman Benneila:(Tunisia)

All Hamady could hear was the grating sound of sirens. He had recoiled in horror and his heart was beating frantically. The explosion had set his ears ringing. His mouth was dry and his eyes roamed around the scene. A moment ago, he had been almost run over by a car driving directly towards him at full speed. It was the second time he had found himself at the brink of death that day. He wiped a stray tear from his cheek and started recalling the events of earlier that day. For instance, Roberto's hug. They would probably remain etched in his mind for a long time.

Maria, Emilio, Sofia...later, they would be recognized for their bravery.

He felt proud of them. Now, it all seemed like a distant nightmare. He took a cigarette out of the packet he carried in his pants pocket, placed it between his lips, lit it, drew on it and swallowed its poison. Then, he exhaled the smoke, which slowly billowed its way to the sky. His body loosened up and a chill slid up his spine.

Just before everything went down, he had been standing on the second floor of the Bardo National Museum with a party of Italian tourists. He was their guide, the one in charge of telling them the stories behind each and every museum piece. Suddenly, he heard what he imagined to be a piece of ceiling plummeting to the ground. At least, that is what he told the tourists in an attempt to calm them down. However, they seemed to disagree with his interpretation of the alarming sound. They were convinced that they were under a terrorist attack. Hamady didn't want to believe them, but he couldn't refute it after he ran towards the stairs leading down to the lower floors, gripped the banister, looked down, and, with his own eyes, saw the bullet holes on the museum walls. He ducked to avoid being seen, and so did the tourists around him. He looked at Maria, who had followed him, together with some of the group. Her eyes were bloodshot and bugging out of their sockets. She was holding her hand against her mouth in an effort to restrain her impulse to scream. Everybody crouched behind the banister, paralyzed by fear.

Suddenly, an idea popped into Hamady's head. He stood up, signalling his group to follow him. They left the building through the closest emergency exit. The bus driver was surprised to see them racing toward him. Hamady saw bullet shells lying on the ground. He picked some of them up. One of the terrorists showed up and began running toward them. As soon as everyone had gotten into the bus, Hamady told the driver to take them to La Goulette. Once they had left the scene and were seemingly out of danger, Hamady started to regain awareness of the world around him. With a shaking hand, he felt through his vest pocket the bullet shells he had just picked up. He took them out and sniffed their smell. Horror gripped him once again.

Once they arrived at the port, he dug a small hole in the earth surrounding a palm tree that had been planted in the middle of the street, and buried the bullet shells in it. As he continued walking, a bright smile flickered across his face.

Peace settled in his heart. He promised himself that he wouldn't let anyone scare him like that in the future.

XVIII
Lake Tritonis

Written by Amina Zaoui.(Tunisia)

Gilisia is a magical land that is said to have been forged by the wind from Eden that Eve stole when she was banished together with our father Adam to God's backyard. Afterward, it was inherited by the descendants of her pious children.

The story goes that this idyllic spot was controlled by a ferocious dragon with insatiable bloodlust. Everyone shuddered with horror; fear stroke into people's hearts and spread throughout the realm like cancer. The harsh punishments meted out to the nation made people lose their strength and lashed them into serfdom. They endured the humiliation in deathly silence and competed against one another to cater to the dragon's demand for the most precious goods such fertile land had to offer. They delivered until the sources had been drained almost to the last drop. They roamed through green and yellow fields up to the point where their legs would hold their weights no longer.

They had no wealth left and fell sick from pure exhaustion. Their silence shattered their dreams and those who had been hoping to throw the dragon off a cliff to crush the injustice and reveal the truth before the flames it shot out of its mouth burned everything to the ground had their patience torn asunder by their fear.

The moment arrived when the misery simply became unbearable and someone decided to show some courage by rising up and challenging his grim fate. However, it didn't just stop there, because his intrepid actions had kindled a revolution, which was now racing through the veins of the oppressed. They gathered and built up alliances until they formed one single body ready to take down any opposition they might encounter. Thereupon, the dragon surrendered and deemed it wise to retreat to a mountain lying in a far-off corner of the world. Every single soul rejoiced at the pleasant-tasting victory and the regained freedom. Surges of elation overflowed across the realm once again.

However, it was not long before they were ablaze with fury. They assembled, discussed, argued, and finally agreed on the importance of appointing another tyrant willing to make them savor their fears and proclivity for feeling degraded. That's how the time-worn ghoul was elected to sit on the throne of the dingy kingdom.

Over the course of the elections, everyone swore to refrain from revealing the truth and to silently pray to God for him to prolong the abomination's life.

Sitting by the shore of Lake Tritonis was Sathania, the beauty of the realm, surrounded by her maids. Butterflies fluttered around the palms of her hands and flowers bent over to listen to the sad tune of her ballads while tears glistening with the sheen of pearls rolled down her marmoreal cheeks.

As soon as the mischievous trout Shansouma realized how much pain her friend was in, she didn't hesitate to ask her for the reason behind all her suffering. Sathania sighed and poured out her heart to her.

"Haven't you heard about the outrageous tragedy that has befallen the country now that the ghoul has drifted into a deep sleep?"

The trout sighed before answering with a quavering voice, "The birds from Gilisia told us about the atrocities the ravens have perpetrated, which have set the whole country on fire."

Silence reigned. Subsequently, the old turtle raised her voice and said, "Legend has it that this earth is doomed to die the moment blood is spilled on the ground."

Fear stepped up Sathania's heartbeat, causing her to shiver. She allowed her imagination to show her the savagery that had just swept the country and could not help but burst into tears again. Her sob of despair split their hearts.All of a sudden, a violent riot erupted in the lake. Raven troops approached, dragging the bodies of humans that had fallen prey to them up the shore, where they thereupon killed them all.

Immediately afterward, a strong wind picked up. It made the trees quiver and the birds fall from the sky as if they were junk.

The blood shed generated loud red waves, which slowly flooded the grassland and dyed the crystal-clear waters of the lake. The gale-force wind howled and made every being shake with fear. It buffeted the small kingdom, drying up rivers and lakes and searing conscience. All signs of life ceased and the lake was replaced with a salty soil that drowned anyone who, unaware of the secret it kept, dared to step over it. At its edge now stretch vast tracts of barren desert land only inhabited by the fata morgana of a beauty bathing in the lake.

XIX
Round Trip

Written by Salah Maaty.(United Arab Emirates)

My brother Kamal wanted me to make the most of my stay in the Emirates, so, on the very first day after landing, he took me on a trip to Sharjah. What struck me most about Sharjah was how well-behaved, culturally-aware and respectful of the Islamic traditions its residents appeared to be compared to Dubai, which is rather a cosmopolitan city that thrives on the work of those who partake in business for pleasure. Because of the position Kamal held at the paper he worked for, which was no other than Al Khaleej Times, people recognized him on the street. After spending the whole day wandering around the city, I started getting tired. My brother noticed it at once and suggested that we return home. The road to Umm al-Quwain was bumpy, and in taking it, we were ignoring the risks it posed at our own peril. One such risk was bumping into one of the herds of wild and untethered camels that traversed the inhospitable deserts, running to and fro with little warning of their arrival.

Back home, Siham, my brother's wife, told us that the National Bank of Umm Al Qaiwain, where I had recently been employed, had launched an investigation against me for disclosing classified information and selling company secrets to a competitor.That news marked a very transformational moment in my fortune. Apparently, important documents that I had hidden had now come to light. It was a given that my boss had already fired me and I had to get back to Egypt immediately.

In the plane, I sat next to an elderly man with a wispy white beard. At some point during the flight, he mumbled out loud, "Our destiny is written down for us."

I turned toward him to ask whether he was addressing me and saw him shaking his head. With a glazed look in his eyes, he resumed, "That's what people say when they feel overwhelmed."

I rejoined with a mirthless smile, "And yet, everyone here seems to be as happy as a clam."

He let out an amused laugh and replied, "Don't let looks deceive you, son. Most people don't like to return home, no matter what their countenances lead you to believe."

Looking directly in his eyes, I asked, "Have our paths crossed before? I feel as if you were talking about me!"

He laughed and, as he stroked his beard, he answered, "I am like the Genie in the Lamp. I have lived in this region for over twenty years and know all its secrets."

The serenity in his voice and his relaxed manner encouraged me to share my story with him. When I finished, he shook his head anew and said, "Boy, you need to accept that everything happens for a reason. The fact that you left Egypt to move to Umm Al Qaiwain, only to board a plane back home not long after, tells me that your behavior obeys the logic of the vicious circles in which the nature of life comes into expression."

"I just want to know the truth!" I uttered, "Who stole the files? Who squealed to the boss?"

"What's the point in knowing? God's ways are beyond our understanding."

At that point, I assumed that we had run out of conversation. I smiled politely and began to picture my wife and daughter waiting for my plane to land at the airport. I missed them. I took my cassette player out of my bag, put in the headphones and pressed play. I was expecting to hear the tape my wife and daughter had recorded, so that I would feel closer to them and less lonely by listening to it while abroad, but instead, another somewhat familiar voice came out of the device. It was Siham's, and it sounded as if she were talking to a friend on the phone. Her voice was clearly audible:

"Nour, I am so happy he is out of my sight, you can't even begin to imagine—it's a real load off my mind. After four months of unbearable stress, I finally plucked up the courage to do what was necessary to kick him out of our lives. I took all his zealously-guarded files from his bag and turned them over to his boss at the bank. Good thing nobody found out and only God can judge me."

I couldn't believe my ears. For a second, I felt as if the plane was about to plummet to the ground with me inside of it. I woke the Genie, who had dozed off a few minutes earlier, to bring him up to speed with the story of my life:

"Genie, I know who stole my files and ratted me out. I've found out who it was!"

The Genie smiled and turned to look at me with his penetrating eyes.

"So what? You weren't meant to stay in the Emirates. That ship has sailed and this one is about to land. Let it be."

I took the tape from the cassette player and laid it on my lap. We were already flying over Egypt. A few minutes later, an announcement came over the speakers stating that we were about to land. The plane made its descent and we arrived on the landing strip. We stood up and walked toward the exit. As I was about to step out of the plane, I heard a voice calling me from behind:

"Sir, I believe this tape belongs to you; it was lying on your seat."

A stewardess was handing me the tape that proved who had destroyed my professional integrity. Right before I was about to stretch out my arm and grab it, I changed my mind, flashed her a smile and said,

"Sorry, it's not mine."

XX

Stairway to Heaven

Written by Anwar Muhammad Alseraggi.(Yemen)

I walk down crowded alleys trying to dodge the fireballs the sun flings at us humans as soon as it has made itself comfortable in the canopy of heaven. The pungent aroma of incense that wafts toward me smacks of the past. I take my time climbing up the seemingly never-ending stairs. The stone steps have been worn smooth by all the people who have traced this route before me.

I stop to look around. The views during the ascent never cease to amaze me. The buildings' facades are adorned with stucco arabesques that crown the wooden windows.

Their bright whiteness resembles that of the jilbabs kids wear. They stand in stark contrast to the rest of the colors of the facades, and to me, they look like the halos of stars. They definitely invite observers to sneak a peek at building interiors.

There is a stunning girl leaning out of one of the windows of a building opposite me. She has big almond eyes and scarlet cheeks. She is wearing a dreamy expression as her gaze drifts down the streets and her braids swing with the morning breeze. On my way to the top, she recedes from view every time I pass one of the windows that is spaced along the side of the tower that faces her, and each time I fear I might have lost her for good. Thus, I pick up my pace.

When the only way up is a spiraling path, one has to tread firmly to put one's mind at ease about moving in the right direction despite the spinning motion. However, when I hear the neighborhood children laugh and the elderly utter their morning prayers, all my fears subside, for my mind reassures me that everything's in its proper place and that I have always—since the beginning of time—belonged here. I feel loved and wanted.

The certainty of being exactly where I am supposed to be boosts my confidence and pushes me to conquer the world.

I move forward by inertia as my feet take me to the most popular café in these parts. It's located on the ninth floor, and it boasts a magnificent view of the entire city. I sit down on a wooden chair whose design matches that of the surrounding architecture and order a coffee.

The waiter brings it to me, and I start drinking it in sips while watching the city rise and wipe the sleep from its eyes. Another day lies ahead, offering the beast that hides behind the appearance of a beauty another shot at turning our lives upside down.Against all odds, she is still there. A blustery wind has picked up and is buffeting at her face. Her braids flutter like the wings of a sparrow that has been caught up in a cyclone.

She seems intent on beguiling me. She entices me to stand up, leave the café, and go for a walk around the city. I lean out of the balcony and contemplate the surrounding buildings. The masterfully crafted, colorful arched windows would add distinction to any edifice and thus raise the already magnificent buildings they are a part of to a whole new category, making them worthy of being considered architectural gems.

The city's splendor blinds me, and for a moment, I lose sight of the girl with braided hair. I am so afraid of losing her again that I lock my gaze on her. In fact, I am so fixated on the girl that I forget about my own two feet, lose balance, and almost fall. I then cast another look at Sanaa's old city.The girl, the café, where am I? What happened to you, Sanaa?

The grandeur of your old buildings attests to your level of advancement and impact once upon a time. But now those glorious times seem to be long gone. Building windows are covered in dust, and the air is filled with the stench of death. In this urban jungle that you have become, life is merely a matter of survival.

XXI

Clutches of Inner Turmoil

Written by Asma Mansoor Al-Menhali.(United Arab Emirates)

Here I am, writing as usual.

I want to reveal what tears me up inside, but I am crippled by horror. I want to pour out my heart, but all my attempts seem doomed to fail. Every time I take a step in that direction, icy, brisk, bitter winds slap my face. I am buffeted by the scourge of my convulsive feelings, which are impervious to the meanings of peace and tranquility, the two states of mind I am so desperate to find myself in.

Here I am, looking for you once again.

I love to write while you are by my side. True to your nature, in spite of being seemingly calm seconds ago, you suddenly fly into a rage.

You distance yourself from me; however, don't dawdle before returning to me anew. Your soft voice has the power to calm my spirit and dispel my worries when I feel edgy and turn to you. Time has elapsed and destiny has ripped my dreams to shreds, dressed me to become its puppet, and left me sapped of energy and life, unable to stand the strain.

Every time we run into each other, you take me to a new place, a different world we own where we can live with nothing to fear. A world where we have cherished hope.

I have missed you so much! You have been the only one capable of comforting me. The numen inside of you draws me close to you, as if it were hoping to allay my suffering with its embrace.

Here I am today to apologize to you for all I have forsaken and forgotten in the past.

I am hereby begging you to save me a place in your depths, for I cannot find serenity if I am not with you. I have already made up my mind and won't regret my choice; that much I promise.

I am willing to leave everything behind me—including this pencil I now hold to express myself—and stride toward you so that you will take me wherever you want us to be together. It will be only a matter of seconds before my frail soul departs for the sky.

You will get to keep my body. Who knows? It may even nourish some fish. It may provide to others what it could not find in itself in order to stay alive, to make it through the cold, dark, sleepless nights. How I yearned at the time for their hugs to keep me warm, for their words to comfort me and make me feel at ease! Yet they shunned me, forsook me, and forgot me.

Now it is my turn.

I am the one leaving, spurning their invitation to continue among them. I will dive in waters far from their reach where I'll finally be able to shake off my painful and abiding memories of them. I will sail over to a place lying far off the shore where their cruelty resides.

I won't let them fool me with their hollow promises any longer—not ever again. This time it'll be me weighing anchor with my sights set on an extrasolar port.

Here I stand before you, the big blue ocean, the one and only, as you sing to me with your welcoming lullaby. Without hesitation, I walk toward you.

This time I won't break my promise to you. I will stay in your snug abyss forever. Take my body and free it from my weak soul.

Take my body and free it from my weak soul.

XXII
Excused

The Author, Hassan Choutam:(Morocco)

I saw him enter the school through a side door and head toward the classroom. I heard one of my students whisper from behind, “It’s Ziad’s dad!”

He was rather short, but strongly-built, and must have been about 50. In the solemn tone of voice his son adopted to answer questions in class, he greeted me and asked where he could find the principal’s office. I asked him why he needed to speak to the principal and he told me he had to take his son out of school. I immediately thought that he would need some kind of divine intervention to get the principal to agree to that, but I wasn’t going to be the one to dash his hopes—it wasn’t my place—so I chose instead to remain silent, smile at him and point him toward the principal’s office. People have the right to entertain hope. He, however, must have read the skepticism in my face, because he proceeded to offer me the context needed to understand his decision.

"The rose fields that surround this beautiful town have certainly turned it into a prosperous tourist destination," he stated. "My wife and I, however, suffer from severe asthma and the roses contribute to aggravating our conditions. It is a shame we have to leave after all the time, money and effort we have invested into these fields, but we cannot risk sharing the same fate my father suffered. He also had asthma and died not long ago from working the fields."

Enter Caption

His revelation left me speechless. He took notice of my reaction and said, in order to cushion the blow, "It's not the end of the world. Zagora is supposed to be a nice place to live in as well. You are most welcomed to come visit any time!"

It took me a few minutes to collect myself and enter the classroom after Ziad's father left. I didn't want the children to see how baffled I was, because I knew they would feel urged to bombard me with questions I didn't have the answers to.

Was moving somewhere else not a betrayal of one's origins? How could anyone choose to trade the roses of Tazakht, namely, what is supposed to represent hope, for the searing heat of the desertic Zagora, which undisputedly stands for despair? How are we to sort out our priorities?

What is more important: our identity, a chance to fulfill ourselves, our place in society, our gender, our financial security, our affectional stability, ...? Is it that reprehensible to leave behind the place you were born in if that is your only way to survive?

One thing was certain: I would miss Ziad. He was one of the smartest kids in my class.

XXIII

Life on Earth Should Come First

Written by Abdul Majeed Taam.(Morocco)

Leila was just over forty and her husband was still madly in love with her. He had never stopped feeling attracted to her, even though her body (having gone through three childbirths) didn't look exactly the same as it had when they first got married. He made sure she knew how much he appreciated her by showering her with compliments on a regular basis. All things considered, one could say Leila had no reason whatsoever to complain about life, considering she had a doting prince-charming-like husband by her side. That is why, when she began to flinch from his touch every time he tried to show her affection, became squeamish about enjoying life for the sake of it, began to pray often and intensely, and eventually to shun human contact, he suspected something had gone terribly wrong.

Leila's strange behavior began after she decided it was about time she learned to read and write. She started attending classes at an institute with adult education programs designed to combat illiteracy among the female population. There, once a week, women of all ages were given lessons for free, on the alphabet and—because the teacher, out of the kindness of her heart, offered to pep up all that dry technical knowledge she had to impart with advice on a subject of a slightly more practical nature—also on the standards of decency.

One day, this overly solicitous teacher told her students that all of God's creations had an expiration date, and women were no exception.

"While they are still young, men are allowed to prey on women and play with them to their hearts' content, but after they have reached the age of forty, men are to stay away from them," she said.

The class started chuckling nervously, wondering whether they were meant to take these observations seriously. Dispelling all doubt, the teacher resumed. "After their wombs have dried up, there is no point in keeping their men's interest in them alive. They should slowly distance themselves from their husbands in order to get closer to God. From then on, they should devote their time to fasting, praying and exhibiting exemplary behavior."

These words left a deep impression on Leila, who from that day on felt it her duty to become an ice queen who wouldn't let her husband's honeyed words melt her resolve to conduct herself the way mid-aged women apparently should. First, she acquired a false veneer of composure to mask her inner conflict. She didn't want anybody to take advantage of her hesitancy; to try and sway her decision on whether or not she should thenceforth set her sights on increasing her odds of entry into the heavenly kingdom. On the one hand, she didn't want to destroy the intimacy she enjoyed with her husband in order to please God. On the other hand, she didn't want to infuriate God and risk losing the appeal she held for her husband.

The teacher's admonition continued ringing in her ears. "Women on earth hold their value until they are forty, but in heaven, their value never expires. For that reason, you, my girls, have to focus on getting into Paradise after you have reached that age when you are no longer capable of reproduction and thus no longer useful to the living."

It didn't take Leila long to realize that her arguments to ignore her age and contravene God's will were untenable.

Meanwhile, Leila's husband didn't understand why his wife was pushing him away. At some point he decided to ask her directly.

"Why are you constantly trying to avoid me lately? Has something changed between us? Why won't you let me get close to you anymore? Don't you miss me, the way I have been missing you?"

"Forget what we had," she replied curtly. "From now on, we have to start preparing for the hereafter. I am not worthy of your attentions now that I am passed the age of forty. My heart now belongs to God and God only. Hallowed be His name."

He gently took her hand and ushered her to the bedroom. There, they lay down on the bed and he kissed her tenderly. As he stroked her hair, he said, "Fuck whoever told you that you were not worthy of my affection! I love you, more than words can express. And I need you here by my side. Please, do this for me. Wait to live for the afterlife until you find yourself in it."

Her face lit up with joy and, after pressing a reassuring kiss on his lips, she fell asleep in his arms. She would never return to class at that institute.

XXIV

The Days of Yore

Written by Ahmed Sana.(Algeria)

White clouds scud across the sky. Peace and quiet reign supreme. The sun is shining. It's a beautiful fall morning and Khaled is wearing a happy smile on his face as he wends his way through the old city. He has gone out to buy antiquities and look at the old houses of the neighborhood. That's the only thing that keeps him distracted from the unbearable sorrow of having lost his dear friend. He has only recently found the strength to leave the house again. His friend's demise has hit him hard, perhaps because of how unexpected it has been.

As he strolls down the Street of the World, he starts to mull over what it is that makes something deserve a certain name. “Take this street, for instance,” he says to himself. “It’s a pretty narrow street, but still, it seems to contain everything that makes the world a miserable place: beggars, thieves, mercenaries, traitors, tourists, neets, ...” It is his all-time favorite street to peek on the bright side of life, especially in the fall. After all, misery loves company.

He likes to see himself as Oedipus, the one with swollen feet. Some might think he is being childish when he sighs and refuses to let go of the past, but that’s only because they can’t fathom how hard it is. They used to embark on adventures, he and his friend; steal oranges and listen to preachers.He might have to retire early to devote himself to reminiscing full time. He knows it is unlikely things will ever return to how they were far back in the mists of time, but hope is beyond doubt always the last to die.

XXV Oud Fragrance

Written by Noor Jasim al-Bakheet.(Kuwait)

The family, consisting of the father, the mother and the two girls, Nur and Zeinab, joined the grandmother, Mariam, around the dinner table. The exquisite fragrance of the spinach pies on the table made Nur's mouth water. She knew her grandmother had baked them with her in mind. As soon as everyone was seated, she lunged over the table to claim a slice of the pie. She didn't, however, gauge her impetus and hit the plate, which landed on the ground and broke into pieces. Her father got his dander up because he knew how precious that specific plate with a design of golden flowers was to his mother, for it had been handed down to her by her own mother. It was the plate on which she always served the spinach pies. He raised his arm to strike the one he deemed responsible for his rage, and she dove for cover to the feet of her grandmother. Nur sank her head in her grandmother's lap and started crying. Her grandmother then got mad at her own son and cursed the plate that had brought her precious granddaughter to tears.

Thirty years had gone by since that happened and her grandmother was already in a better place, but she still recalled the incident in detail. The oud aroma brought the memory back to her, for that was what her grandmother smelled of when she, in a desperate attempt to avoid having her father's iron discipline administered to her, plunged into her arms. She felt so secure back then, enveloped in the sweet oud fragrance, that, for a second, she wished she could stay there forever and it would never fade away. As far as she could remember, her grandmother always wore oud perfume, so much so, that, as a small child, she believed the oud aroma to be her natural body odor, the one grandmothers have. It wasn't until she grew a little older and started attending school that she learnt from her classmates that grandmothers aren't necessarily supposed to smell of oud. For her fifteenth birthday, her grandmother gave her the bottle of oud fragrance she had used her entire life and told her to take good care of it, for that bottle was almost as dear to her as she, her granddaughter, herself.

Every Friday, the whole extended family would gather at her grandmother's, including her and her sister's neighborhood peers. Even her uncle drove down sometimes from the remote city where he lived with his family, and she got to see her cousins and have a blast playing with them. Her grandmother was usually the one to keep an eye on the children. After the meal, she always gave them some money to rush to the candy store and buy some neon-colored tongue-dyeing popsicles.

Grandmother's place was always full of different aromas, like that of mint, which she grew in her backyard, and that of cinnamon and cardamom, which wafted out from the kitchen. On top of that, she liked to wave burning incense sticks around the house to ward off the evil spirits that, according to her, envy gave rise to. She would carefully place them inside the keyholes of every door and put a bucket underneath them, so that the ash would fall inside, lest the dying embers set the expensive carpet on fire. Even the cats from the neighborhood competed for her love, which she expressed to them by letting them have the leftovers of her last meal.

Whenever she felt like indulging in fantasies of a wild nature, Nur liked to drape herself over the rocking chair, which still smelled of her grandmother. It was the last piece of furniture they had rescued from her old house. She wished the time machine had actually been invented. That way she could have acquired one to go back to when they would all join her grandmother around the dinner table. Just being able to return to her grandmother's humble abode in order to escape the frenzied pace of her life for a while would have sufficed though.

I return from my reveries and go to my room, where I catch a whiff of the oud perfume emanating from the bottle she once gave me as a gift. The world is still a beautiful place.

Thank You

THE END

9 798885 036856

Printed by Libri Plureos GmbH in Hamburg,
Germany